PORTRAIT OF
LOCH LOMOND
& THE TROSSACHS
NATIONAL PARK

ANDY STANSFIELD

HALSGROVE

First published in Great Britain in 2008

Title page: **Loch Voil in summer**
In the very heart of Breadalbane lies Loch Voil, on the north side of which the Braes of Balquhidder (right) were
once tramped by Rob Roy MacGregor (1671–1734), immortalised in 1817 by the publication of Sir Walter Scott's novel.

British Library Cataloguing-in-Publication Data
A CIP record for this title is available from the British Library

ISBN 978 1 84114 796 3

HALSGROVE
Halsgrove House,
Ryelands Industrial Estate,
Bagley Road, Wellington, Somerset TA21 9PZ
Tel: 01823 653777 Fax: 01823 216796
email: sales@halsgrove.com
website: www.halsgrove.com

Printed and bound by Grafiche Flaminia, Italy

INTRODUCTION

The author is often asked about the process of visiting and recording visually the area covered by a book, and how decisions are taken about what to include and what to leave out. There is no simple answer which can be applied to every commission other than that, in the end and for this particular photographer, gut instinct determines the choice of what is photographed and what isn't. That instinct relies on an initially subconscious assessment of the very essence of the subject, one which is probably not even put into words until after the project is completed. This is why, although the reader will peruse the introduction before leafing through the book, in actual fact the author will generally only write the introduction at the end of the whole process.

So how does this particular author sum up the essence of the Loch Lomond and The Trossachs National Park? It is not so much terribly beautiful as a place of terrible beauty. Had my visits been made only in summer, the answer might have been different. The mountains seem much more accessible then and the lochs more inviting, a cooling influence on the vibrant colours of a sunlit summer landscape. But I visited the area throughout the year, as indeed do many visitors, and winter adds a very different dimension to the landscape: one of caution and hardship. Winter is not a period of rest, it is a time for both Man and Nature to rise to the challenge.

A place of terrible beauty.

It is always interesting to see how others interpret the landscape, a term I always use in its widest sense to include both present day and historical factors, both natural and human influences. When this National Park was undergoing the process of designation, a number of renowned artists and sculptors were commissioned to create works of art within it to celebrate its creation.

Each made their own assessment of the essence of the area, in some cases very different from my own. They all based their completed works on natural aspects of the area, though some also introduced modern technology into the way they told the story of the landscape. The most sustainable of these projects 'reflects current forestry policy' and involves the harvesting of Sitka spruce to make waterproof matches, with each felled tree being replaced by the planting of two more, eventually restoring some of the native woodland.

A totally different approach was taken by two artists who combined forces to place 30 sculpted SMS receivers on trees in order to receive text messages of love and display them on small LED screens. A modern day equivalent of carving the initials of your loved one into the bark of a tree. Each to his own. I use modern technology to interpret and record the landscape but don't happen to believe in being intrusive in that process.

There are lots of places around the National Park where its interpretation is made easier for visitors, especially in the southern and eastern areas. The Park has its own visitor centres on Lomond Shores at Balloch, at Luss and at Balmaha, on the western and eastern shores of Loch Lomond respectively. The Trossachs Discovery Centre can be found in Aberfoyle and the Breadalbane Folklore Centre is located in Killin, both focusing on their own specific parts of the Park, and there is also the Rob Roy and Trossachs Visitor Centre in Callander.

But the western area of the National Park remains more of a mystery. It is less frequently visited, largely because access is less direct and, with the obvious exception of Benmore Botanic Gardens, it offers less in the way of services for travellers and tourists. The defining of the boundary here, always a contentious issue, is also a mystery in places, particularly with regard to land owned by the Ministry of Defence along Glen Douglas. Nevertheless, the western parts of the Park give access to the sea lochs which bring their own unique rewards of sightings of seals and porpoises and flocks of waders.

Every square mile contains something of value, a feature worth preserving, and that makes for at least 720 different locations which deserve to be included in this book. We haven't gone quite that far but hopefully the images which follow will tempt you to visit a wider selection of locations on future visits.

Andy Stansfield

LOCATION MAP – Loch Lomond

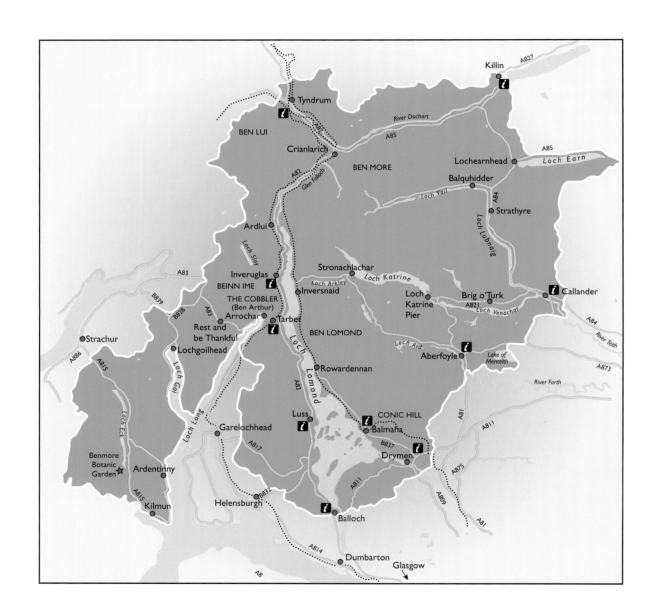

Reflection
Ben Lomond and summer skies reflected in the gently rippling waters of Loch Lomond.

Atmosphere
Loch Lomond provides a huge variety of photo opportunities and not just in brilliant sunshine.

Loch Ard
To the west of Aberfoyle, along the road to Stronachlachar and Inversnaid,
this beautiful loch provides one of the best views of Ben Lomond.

Rest and be Thankful
This memorial at the top of the pass above Glen Croe commemorates the
construction of the military road in the aftermath of the Jacobite Rebellion in 1765.

Left:
High Glencroe
Glen Croe looking west from the road up to Rest and be Thankful.

Mountain stream at Dukes Pass
Run-off from the hills tumbles down this stream after a night of heavy rain.

Sculpture
Stark contrast between the softness of the landscape and the sharp edges of slabs of rock
hewn from the hillside at the start of the 3 Lochs Forest Drive just north of Aberfoyle.

Evening light over Loch Lomond
View from Loch Lomond Shores, the generic name for the collection of visitor services at Balloch, which includes the National Park information centre, café and shopping facilities and visits aboard the *Maid of the Loch*.

Left:
Tarbet Isle, Loch Lomond
The rich greens of the pine trees on Tarbet Isle contrast with the rust colours of bracken on the hillside above the far shore.

All ashore
On a cruise up Loch Katrine you can alight here at Stronachlachar, where there are basic services, and cycle back on bikes hired at the same time you buy your cruise tickets.

Right:
Loch Katrine
Known mainly for its loch cruises, especially on the steamship *Sir Walter Scott*, this loch is only accessible by road at two points: Stronachlachar and the cruise terminus at its eastern end.

11th century Viking grave

Ancient gravestones at Luss

The churchyard at Luss, on the western shore of Loch Lomond, contains a number of interesting old gravestones including a rare 11th century hog-backed Viking grave. Several churches have occupied this site as far back as 520 AD and the era of St Kessog, to whom the present church is dedicated.

Luss

This is a fascinating conservation village portrayed as Glendarroch in Scottish Television's series *High Road*.

Achray Forest and Ben A'an
The subdued colours of the hillside are given emphasis by the patch of lingering low cloud over the loch below.

Light and shade
Dramatic lighting shows the sheer variety of landscape scenery on a winter's day in the Trossachs.

Ben Arthur
Dramatic winter lighting picks out the snow on Ben Arthur
(884m), better known as The Cobbler.

Right:
Loch Arklet
This stunning panorama awaits as you reach Loch Arklet, with views from left
to right of A' Chrois (848m), Beinn Ime (1011m) and Ben Vane (915m).

View from Drymen
The village of Drymen lies in the south east of the National Park.
Opposite the Buchanan Arms Hotel a footpath leads to this viewpoint.

Left:
Drymen Bridge and Endrick Water
Close to Drymen, Endrick Water passes beneath this
attractive bridge and forms a classic series of meanders.

Tigh na Mor in summer
Undoubtedly one of the author's favourite lochs, Loch Achray is surrounded by tumbling hillsides filled with a huge variety of tree shapes and colours, at the foot of which is the former hotel of Tigh na Mor which resembles a French château.

Left:
Tigh na Mor in winter
The colours change but the location is just as captivating.

Loch Doine
Deep in the heart of Breadalbane, this winter scene shows how colourful the hillsides can be,
despite the wintry covering of the mountains in the distance.

A landscape in the making
Ten thousand years ago this scene was scoured by a thick ice sheet. Today the trickle of mountain streams begin to carve shallow gullies, identifiable by their shadows in the strong side-lighting, like the two which merge just above this lochside cottage.

River Leven
At the southern end of Loch Lomond, Balloch is the main mooring place for recreational boats as well as a departure point for cruises around the loch.

Meeting point
The River Leven and Loch Lomond come together in this tranquil location just north of Balloch.

Mountainside
This mountainside between Balquhidder and Inverlochlarig rebuffs the assumption that conifer plantations are shapeless expanses of dark green.

Bonsai
The places in which trees can take hold never ceases to amaze.

Balmaha
This small community on Loch Lomond's eastern shore benefits from sheltered moorings,
a National Park Visitor Centre and a highly recommended menu at the local inn.

Dinghies at Balmaha
There are many places around Loch Lomond in particular, but also at other lochside locations
in the National Park, where visitors can hire a variety of craft to explore local shores.

Winter visitors
The National Park is a year round attraction for visitors
from all over the world.

Right:
Cruise ships
Moored off the village of Tarbet on Loch Lomond's western shore,
these vessels provide a variety of cruises around the loch.

View from Luss
Luss has a small pier on an attractive bay with uninterrupted views of Ben Lomond, but it is also
worthwhile exploring the several inland walks from this interesting village, all of which are detailed in
a free leaflet. These walks explore the remains of former weaving and quarrying communities.

Luss Pier
This image of Luss was taken from the shore, just north of the village, on The Camping & Caravanning Club site.
The author's tent was pitched just 20ft from the water's edge with staggering views available all day long.

Benmore Botanic Garden
With footpaths within the gardens totalling in excess of six miles, Benmore can occupy an entire day.
It has some of the tallest trees in the UK, over 250 species of rhododendron, and separate areas devoted to plants
which grow in other parts of the world, such as Bhutan, but which flourish in the micro-climate here.

Left:
Rhododendrons and Loch Goil
These prolific plants are by far the most common show of colour around the
National Park but this area near Lochgoilhead is one of the prettiest.

Renewable energy

The notion of sustainable energy sources is far from new. This hydro-electric power station on the western shore of Loch Lomond at Inveruglas is fed by water from Loch Sloy, hidden high above in the hills. The water travels 3km along a tunnel right through Ben Vorlich (943m) before being piped down the hillside. The dam on Loch Sloy was constructed by German prisoners of war and the power station, the largest of its kind in the UK, was opened by The Queen in 1950.

Right:
A' Chrois
Looking westwards towards A' Chrois (848m) from Inveruglas and the power station.
Pylons can be seen on the right carrying electricity up to Loch Sloy and the dam.

Tarbet Isle
One of two dozen islands surrounded by the waters of Loch Lomond, this one takes its name from the nearest village of Tarbet. Vikings are said to have dragged their longships overland the short distance from Loch Long and Arrochar, at the head of the sea loch, to Tarbet so they could explore Loch Lomond.

Right:
Ben Lomond and Tarbet Isle
This attractive island stands out against the mountain, deep in shadow, in the early evening light.

Loch Long
The head of Loch Long with the outskirts of Arrochar just visible in the distance.

Loch Long and The Cobbler
South of Arrochar, as the road to Loch Lomond climbs up towards Glen Douglas, it affords a sweeping view over
Loch Long and the mountains beyond, including from right to left A' Chrois (848m), Beinn Narnain (926m) and
The Cobbler (884m) or Ben Arthur to give it its proper name.

Bracken
The deep rust colour of dead bracken is enriched further
by low afternoon light.

Left:
Loch Lomond sunrise
Being surrounded by mountainous terrain, opportunities for
sunsets casting a glow over the loch are limited but looking
south east on a winter morning can be equally rewarding.

Plantation and snow
The densely forested slopes of Sron nan Colan, just outside Tyndrum,
contrast starkly with the snow clad summit of Beinn Chuirn (880m).

Glen Falloch
Looking towards Troisgeach (733m) and Beinn Darnhain (684m), heavy cloud shadow reduces the glen to a silhouette.

Glen Fruin
Under normal circumstances this road through Glen Fruin, in the south west of the
National Park, is rarely used. There is a far more substantial road running parallel to it, only a
matter of a hundred yards up the hillside in places, which forms the main road from Loch Lomond over
to Gare Loch and Loch Long. The latter is also the route of choice for 'sensitive' loads being ferried
to the nuclear submarine base at Faslane and the separate Royal Navy armaments depot.

Right:
Glenn Luss
It is easy to miss the road into this lovely glen which gradually becomes more
and more impassable as it climbs to the isolated properties at its head.

Pines in winter
Glen Falloch is well known for its scattering of pines, the remnants of ancient
woodlands which once covered the area, with Ben Glas in the background.

Ben Glas in summer
The craggy summit of Ben Glas (715m) and the nearer slopes of Stob Glas (710m)
guard the northern approach to Loch Lomond from Crianlarich.

Winter colour
The slopes of Loch Lomond are a vivid spectacle on a sunny day, even in winter.

Smoke on the water
Not so much Deep Purple as deep rust, the rich tones of moorland grasses and
bracken are reflected in the still waters of Loch Lomond.

Contre jour
This French expression is used to denote photographs taken into the light, where colour all but disappears, as in this early morning shot of a distant Ben Lomond.

Lake of Menteith
This is the only 'lake' in
Scotland as all others are
named as lochs. There is an
island on the lake called
Inchmahome to which you
can take a ferry and visit
the Priory there.

Reeds
The upward thrust of this small clump of sharply defined reeds contrasts with the horizontal
solidity of the rocky shore and the swirling ill-defined movement of water around it.

Ancient and modern

Following the Jacobite Rebellion of 1745 'redcoat' soldiers constructed a military road from Dumbarton, just north of Glasgow, to Inverary in the western highlands. Today a modern road carries traffic more readily over the pass at Rest and be Thankful. The essentially straight new road can be seen crossing the picture, with the old military road snaking its way down the glen below it.

Butterbridge

On the National Park boundary in Glen Kinglas, this wonderful packhorse bridge can be found adjacent to the main road over Rest and be Thankful to Loch Fyne. It was built immediately after the Jacobite Rebellion to enable the new military road to cross Kinglas Water en route to Inveraray.

The first of the Forth
At the eastern end of Loch Ard its outlet, later to be the River Forth, narrows briefly then opens out into this small pool with the sun sparkling on Ben Lomond in the distance, before continuing its way through Aberfoyle as a clearly defined river.

Loch Ard
To the west of Aberfoyle, along the road to Stronachlacar and Inversnaid,
this beautiful loch provides one of the best views of Ben Lomond.

Loch Ard Forest
Irregular patches of forestry with different levels of maturity provide a much
more attractive view than large expanses of trees of the same age.

Post Bus

In such a remote area with single track roads being the norm, ordinary bus services are just not viable. Instead, there is the post bus which combines two valuable services.

Marion

If it wasn't for the Royal Mail flag flying from its bow, you would never guess that this boat is used by Balmaha's postman to deliver mail to the islands of Loch Lomond. Visitors can join him on his daily round for a small fee.

A' Chrois, Beinn Ime and Ben Vane
These three mountains, viewed from the shores of Loch Arklet, lie beyond Loch Lomond
and are five miles away which gives some idea of their true size.

Below:
Ben Lomond from the south east
One of the most open vistas of Ben Lomond can be had from just south of Aberfoyle.

View from Inversnaid
The grand old hotel at Inversnaid, on the eastern shore of Loch Lomond, lies at the end of the long but dramatic drive from Aberfoyle. The hotel has its own jetty (left).

Dramatic Lighting
The sharp contrast between foreground, middle distance and the snow-capped mountains
gives this view a great sense of depth.

Breadalbane
A plume of smoke is the only hint of human presence in this Trossachs wilderness.

Tourists
The entire National Park is popular with tourists and travellers, with coach tours being one of the favourite ways of seeing its sights.

Pedal power
Cycling is a wonderful way of enjoying the Trossachs scenery, the rigours of the
uphill sections being balanced by thrilling downhill stretches.

Woodland floor
Last autumn's dead leaves, lichens and new shoots make
a colourful picture in spring.

Left:
Loch Katrine cycle route
A cycle track follows the entire northern shore of Loch Katrine,
round the western end of the loch and along its
southern shore as far as Stronachlachar.

Loch Lomond
Lochside trees frame many of the views across Loch Lomond from vantage points along its western shore.

Loch Chon
View westwards over Loch Chon and Beinn Dubh. Behind the ridge lies Gleann Dubh into which drain all the burns from the eastern flanks of Ben Lomond.

Loch Lubnaig and Meall Mor
This loch lies between Callander and Strathyre in the east of the National Park, with
two lochside parking areas at its southern end being popular picnic spots.

Ben Ledi and Stank Glen
An unfortunate name for a very attractive glen on the north side of Ben Ledi (879m), viewed from across Loch Lubnaig.

Clan MacNab burial ground

On the south side of Dochart Bridge in Killin lies this private burial ground. It is open to the public but occasionally the keys to the small access gate need to be collected from Breadalbane Folklore Centre in the old mill just over the bridge.

Clan MacNab burial ground
Clan chiefs were buried here along with members of their close family.

Dochart Bridge
Winter rains and melting snow can create a torrent almost overnight.

Balloch Castle Country Park
The grounds of Balloch Castle lie on the hillside at the south eastern corner of Loch Lomond and provide
a peaceful place to walk while enjoying views over the National Park and Scotland's most famous loch.

Lichens
These rampant lichens make an attractive arrangement, surrounded by rust-coloured dead leaves which highlight the vibrant green strands.

Moss and wall
The hard edges of an ancient stone wall in woodland are softened by a thick carpet of moss.

Loch Arklet
This stunning panorama awaits as you reach Loch Arklet, with views from left to right of
A' Chrois (848m), Ben Vane (915m), Beinn Ime (1011m) and Ben Vorlich (943m).

Loch Venachar
Running east to west between Callander and Loch Katrine, the north shore of Loch Venachar
is easily accessed from the A821 and provides fine views westwards of Ben Venue (727m) and Achray Forest.

Loch Restil
The western boundary of the National Park passes through this shot of Loch Restil,
between the loch and Binnein an Fhidhleir in the centre.

Mirror image
The *Maid of the Loch* is reflected perfectly by the still
waters of Loch Lomond at Balloch.

Left:
Early morning mist
The rising sun provides the backlighting for this shot of the island of
Inchlonaig, one of the larger islands at the southern end of Loch Lomond.

Loch Lomond at its best
The *Maid of the Loch*, snow on Ben Lomond, the still blue waters of
Loch Lomond itself, and Balloch Castle Country Park just visible on the right.

Summer morning
The sun is still hidden behind a bank of cloud but strong enough to light up
the mist over Inchlonaig (left) and the tip of Inchconnachan (right), two of the
larger islands at the southern end of Loch Lomond.

Ben Lomond from Luss
This tranquil February scene shows why the area is popular all year round, especially with walkers and canoeists.

Ben Lomond from Tarbet
The large grassy area in the foreground is a favourite spot for picnics with extensive views
of Ben Lomond and the dense plantation between Cailness and Rowardennan.

The Trossachs Church
This is one of the most photographed churches in Scotland, especially from across the loch.

Right:
Trossachs Church
The Church of Scotland serves the Congregation of Callander Kirk in the most delightful setting imaginable,
perched on a small shelf between this colourful Trossachs hillside and the still waters of Loch Achray.

Adrenaline rush
As well as providing ample climbing and mountain biking opportunities,
the area is popular for some of the more exciting water sports.

Left:
Movie set
The picturesque setting of the Trossachs Church
has been used in several films.

If I just twiddle this . . .
Adults and children alike make the
most of water sports opportunities on
Loch Lomond. Here, a small
adjustment is made to improve
performance.

Dinghies, Loch Lomond
These two dinghies make an
attractive picture against the lush
green reeds in summer.

Balquhidder
In the heart of Breadalbane lies the stamping ground of Rob Roy MacGregor (1671–1734),
immortalised in 1817 by the publication of Sir Walter Scott's novel.

Loch Voil in summer
In the very heart of Breadalbane lies Loch Voil, on the north side of which tower the Braes of Balquhidder (right).

Duck Bay
This quiet stretch of the western shore of Loch Lomond is accessed
by a short stretch of the old road, though you are likely to see more
seagulls than ducks. Today sections of the old road alongside the loch make up
part of a cycle route offering largely traffic-free enjoyment.

Left:
Summer
The season seems to take a long time to arrive and to be all
too short, but when it does arrive it is well worth the wait.

Beinn Dubhchraig in winter
At a respectable height of 978m Beinn Dubhchraig looks a less formidable challenge than craggy Ben Lui (1130m), behind it on the right and shrouded in cloud.

Killin
Beyond the River Dochart rise (from left to right) Beinn nan Eachan (1000m), Meall Garbh (1026m) and
Meall nan Tarmachan (1044m) all of which look deceptively easy climbs on a summer's day.

Ben Lomond from Firkin Point

One of the most fascinating things about Ben Lomond is that it has so many different
profiles when viewed from different locations around the National Park.

Ben Lomond in all its glory
This magnificent mountain looks twice its actual height (974m) in some circumstances.

Hell's Glen

At this point along the road from Rest and be Thankful to Lochgoilhead, a road branches off along Gleann Beag, also known as Hell's Glen. This was the route of the Duke's Road or main transport route from the lowlands to Inveraray and also one of many areas of the highlands stripped of its local population during the infamous sheep clearances.

Loch Achray
The western end of this small but beautiful loch, where the road peels off to Loch Katrine for cruises on the historic SS *Sir Walter Scott*.

Carraig na Maraig and Loch Goil
Viewed from across Loch Goil at Carrick Castle, Carraig na Maraig and nearby Carraig nan Ron form the tip of a large
wild peninsula within the western reaches of the National Park which is completely inaccessible by road.

Loch Goil
Looking northwards along the western shore of this sea loch, which branches off from Loch Long,
towards Cruach nam Miseag (606m) and far right Ben Donich (847m).

The Old Kirk, Balquhidder
Standing next to the present day parish church, for centuries this was the place of
worship for the Clan MacLaren and the final resting place of many Clan Chiefs.

Balquhidder Parish Church

Better known as the location of Rob Roy MacGregor's grave, the church also has an attractive interior and there is a short walk from its tiny car park to the hillside above, providing extensive views over the heart of Breadalbane.

Plaque, The Old Kirk, Balquhidder

Right:
Lochgoilhead and Ben Donich
This small town at the northern end of the loch nestles beneath the brooding
mass of Ben Donich (847m) and the forest which hides Donich Water.

Endangered or dangerous?
Motorists near Inveronich are warned to
be on the lookout for red squirrels.

Left:
Lochgoilhead
As this is a sea loch, watersports enthusiasts take a
breather while waiting for the tide to come in.

Fire break
Extensive areas of forestry are broken by wide gaps to prevent the spread
of fire, like this one on the lower slopes of Stob na Boine.

Right:
Loch Eck
View southwards down Loch Eck, in the western reaches of the
National Park, with Clach Bheinn (643m) in the distance.

Dornoch Point
This promontory jutting defiantly out into Loch Eck at Dornoch Point is popular with wild campers and fishermen alike.

Kilmun Church

Founded in 1442 by Sir Duncan Campbell, who was buried here in 1453, only a ruined tower remains of the original church. The square mausoleum with the domed roof was completed in 1796 and contains the remains of many important members of the Campbell family. The information board outside the church records a macabre tale with a touch of humour: "The Marquis of Argyll, executed for treason in 1661, is buried in the vault. His headless body was taken to Kilmun, while his severed head was displayed around the Kingdom and not reunited with the rest of him until 1664."

119

Elizabeth Blackwell
1821–1910
Also buried at Kilmun Church
is Elizabeth Blackwell, the first
woman to qualify as a doctor.

Kilmun Church

Main street in Aberfoyle
This small town is where you can find the Trossachs Discovery Centre which is well worth a
visit and from which you can pick up an excellent leaflet of walks centred on the town.

Aberfoyle

David Marshall Lodge
Located just outside Aberfoyle off the Dukes Pass road, this Visitor Centre (not to be confused with the Trossachs Discovery Centre in the town centre) serves as the base for exploration of the Queen Elizabeth Forest Park. It has live webcams covering various nests and nesting boxes, including an osprey nest.

Right:
View over Aberfoyle
The houses of Aberfoyle peek through the trees in this view across the
Loch Ard Forest from the hills above the town.

Craigmore

The crags of Craigmore (387m) tower over this delightful pond at the Queen Elizabeth Forest Park Visitor Centre, a peaceful setting for a picnic. The children will be fascinated by the Visitor Centre and can burn off excess energy at 'Go Ape' with its rope ladders, bridges, trapezes and zip wires (minimum age 10yrs).

Lochside camping
It is not unusual to see tents erected on the shores of many lochs in the area, though it's relatively rare for Loch Lomond.

Queen Elizabeth Forest Park
The area can be explored by car using the 3 Lochs Forest Drive which is normally open between Easter and September, though its opening in 2008 was delayed considerably by harvesting difficulties caused by late winter weather. You can check its status by telephoning 01877 382383.

Loch Ard Forest near Aberfoyle
To the south west of Aberfoyle the land is largely flat and covered by the Loch Ard Forest,
bordered by pastures such as this one graced by two beautiful ponies.

Loch Earn looking west
The café and marina at Lochearnhead.

Loch Earn looking east
Taken from the marina at Lochearnhead looking west towards St Fillans. A local tells a fascinating tale of how
Ben Vorlich (985m) to the south can either block weather out or keep it trapped in the vicinity. One evening he
was playing golf in the dry just six miles away at St Fillans, at the opposite end of the loch, while the run-off from
torrential rain tore up road surfaces and flushed away tons of gravel beach at Lochearnhead.

Lady of the Lake
If you miss the boat, literally, when hoping for a cruise around Loch Katrine on the historic steamship *Sir Walter Scott*, the *Lady of the Lake* will be your cruise vessel.

Right:
Stronachlachar
Loch Katrine cruises make a stop here, almost at the western end of the loch, so you can walk or cycle back again. View northwards from the pier, with the dramatic downward sweep of Meall na Boineide on the left and Stob a'Choin (869m) in the background.

Falls of Dochart in summer
In winter torrents of water tumble across these rocks at Killin, where summer visitors can sit basking in the sunshine.

Falls of Dochart in winter
Winter rains and meltwater from February snow on some of the highest mountains in the
National Park swell the River Dochart to create these spectacular falls at Killin.

Glen Dochart in summer

Wild and wonderful in winter
The River Dochart tumbles aimlessly around every obstacle while a rich variety of
plant life clings to every rock, hoping not to be swept away.

Lonesome pine
Opposite the old flax mill which lies adjacent to the A827 in Glen Dochart stands
this magnificent solitary pine on a mound covered with bluebells.

Glen Falloch
The legendary pines of Glen Falloch were once part of the great Caledonian Forest. Today very few remain, standing proudly in small clusters as an elegant reminder of how impressive they were in large numbers.

Falls of Falloch

This waterfall is probably more beautiful in summer than in winter when its fine spray becomes a dramatic torrent.

Cloud shadow, Loch Lomond
This image shows just how dramatic the scenery becomes when the mountains are darkened by shadows created by passing clouds.

Nature's riches
Tiny droplets of glistening rainwater cling to this birch like miniature jewels.

141

**Cloud shadow,
The Trossachs**
The sweeping lines of this
Trossachs landscape are
emphasised by cloud shadow.

Reflection: *Maid of the Loch*

This shot of the famous ship moored at the southern end of Loch Lomond is its reflection turned the right way up – and a final reminder that this National Park is both a recreational paradise and a wilderness to treasure. It's all a matter of how you look at it.